An Imprint of Pop!
popbooksonline.com

American Indians

THE IROQUOIS

by N.C. Barnes

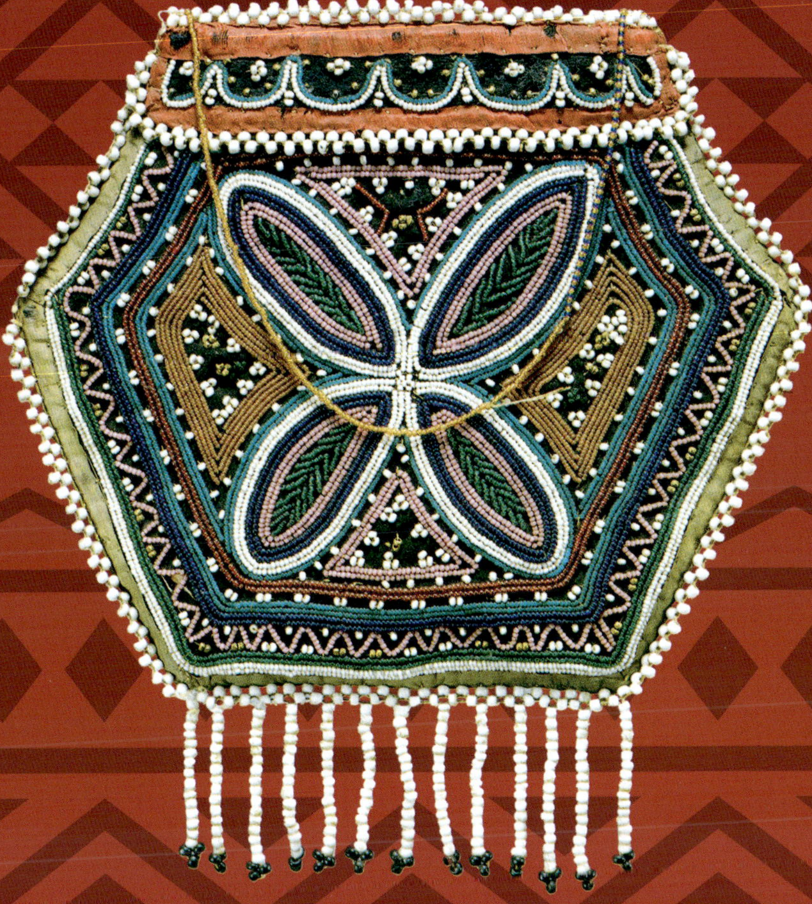

This book is filled with videos, puzzles, games, and more! Scan the QR codes* while you read, or visit the website below to make this book pop.

popbooksonline.com/Iroquois

abdobooks.com

Published by Pop!, a division of ABDO, PO Box 398166, Minneapolis, Minnesota 55439.

Printed in the United States of America, North Mankato, Minnesota.

052024
082024

THIS BOOK CONTAINS RECYCLED MATERIALS

Cover Photo: Getty Images

Interior Photos: Getty Images, Shutterstock Images, Wikimedia, Associated Press, Sailko/Wikimedia, Alamy Stock Photos, Arno Burgi/dpa/picture-alliance/Newscom

Editor: Emily Dreher

Series Designer: Colleen McLaren

Library of Congress Control Number: 2023947502

Publisher's Cataloging-in-Publication Data

Names: Barnes, N.C., author.

Title: The Iroquois / by N.C. Barnes

Description: Minneapolis, Minnesota : Pop!, 2025 | Series: American Indians | Includes online resources and index

Identifiers: ISBN 9781098246211 (lib. bdg.) | ISBN 9781098246778 (ebook)

Subjects: LCSH: Iroquois Indians--Juvenile literature. | American Indians--Juvenile literature. | Indians of North America--Juvenile literature. | Indigenous peoples--Social life and customs--Juvenile literature. | Cultural anthropology--Juvenile literature.

Classification: DDC 973.0497--dc23

*Scanning QR codes requires a web-enabled smart device with a QR code reader app and a camera.

TABLE OF CONTENTS

CHAPTER 1

WHO ARE THE IROQUOIS?

Before European **settlers** came to North America, the land was mostly wild and open. It was populated by American Indians. Each group had its own languages and culture. Culture is the customs, arts, and ideas of a group of people.

WATCH A VIDEO HERE!

The Iroquois people decorated their clothes with seashells.

The Iroquois people are known as the Haudenosaunee. This means "people of the longhouse." Iroquois nations make up the Haudenosaunee Confederacy. It includes the Mohawk, Oneida, Onondaga, Cayuga, and Seneca nations. They make decisions for their people together.

At the center of the Haudenosaunee logo is the Great Tree of Peace.

Men usually built the longhouses.

Among each nation are clans. A clan is made of groups of people who consider each other family. The size of clans varies. Each clan is represented by an animal. Clan membership is passed down from mothers.

DID YOU KNOW?

In 1722, the Tuscarora nation joined the Haudenosaunee Confederacy.

Historically, the Iroquois people lived in what is now Ohio, Pennsylvania, New York, and North Carolina. They also lived in Ontario and Quebec in Canada. This land was forested and filled with streams, rivers, and lakes, including Lake Ontario.

Living around so much fresh water gave the Iroquois all kinds of food.

IROQUOIS HOMELANDS

Leaders consider future generations when they make decisions for their clan.

Clans in the Haudenosaunee are led by Clan Mothers and Chiefs. All nations have a council that makes decisions protecting their people, laws, and traditions. The number of clans in a nation varies.

Some white Americans photographed American Indians to document the culture they thought was fading.

CHAPTER 2

HISTORICAL LIFE

The Iroquois lived in homes known as longhouses. They were long structures built from young trees and tree bark. The houses were usually 18 feet (5.5m) wide and 200 feet (61m) long.

Longhouses had no windows, but they had holes in the roof to let out smoke. There were doors at each end of a longhouse.

Longhouses were traditionally rounded. This is a re-creation.

DID YOU KNOW?

Corn, beans, and squash were known as three sisters because they grow from Mother Earth.

Entire families lived in longhouses. They included an **elder** woman, her husband, their daughters and their husbands, and all their children.

Sleeping platforms were often lined with furs to make them more comfortable.

Longhouses had sleeping platforms along the walls. Home items and corn were hung from above the platforms. Dried squash and beans were stored below.

The Haudenosaunee traveled and fished in canoes made of tree bark.

Men hunted bears, deer, rabbits, ducks, geese, and beavers with bows and arrows and traps. Families took trips to rivers and lakes. There, men fished with lines and nets made from plant fibers and hooks made from bones. Women farmed corn, beans, and squash. They gathered wild roots, fruits, and nuts.

The Haudenosaunee made their clothes and shoes from fur, deerskin, and elk hides. Women wore dresses, skirts, and shirts decorated with porcupine quills. Men wore leather **breechcloths** and *gustoweh*, which are curved wooden hats decorated with eagle feathers. The number of eagle feathers represented which nation they were from.

In the winter, Haudenosaunee people wore deerskin leggings.

CHAPTER 3

TRADITIONS AND FAMILY

Before the Haudenosaunee Confederacy formed, the nations warred with each other. A **prophet** called the Peacemaker came to the Mohawks.

He told them to live peacefully with the other nations. After the Peacemaker proved his wisdom and power, the Mohawks followed his directions. The five nations joined together.

PEACEMAKER

The Peacemaker was sent to the five nations to teach them *Kariwiio,* or "good mind." He also helped organize leadership in each nation. The first person to believe his message was a woman. The Peacemaker decided women should be the most important Haudenosaunee leaders.

The Peacemaker was sent by the Creator. The Creator made everything on Earth.

EXPLORE LINKS HERE!

Chiefs from each Haudenosaunee nation meet from time to time.

When the five nations first joined together, they were called the Great League of Peace. Their **principles** teach people to live peacefully with each other and nature. The Great League of Peace protects Haudenosaunee traditions and the **environment** for future **generations**.

Haudenosaunee children grew up surrounded by family. They were raised and cared for by all the adults in their longhouse. They called every woman "mother" and referred to their cousins as "brother" and "sister."

Children were taught traditions and stories from **elders** in the longhouse. Girls watched their mothers and nature to learn about gathering food, planting and **harvesting** crops, and sewing.

Babies were carried on cradleboards.

Men in a longhouse taught their sons how to trade, hunt, fish, and defend themselves. Men left the home to get married.

Women were the heads of the family. They

Dolls were sometimes made of corn husks.

Clan elders were well respected and considered wise.

stayed at the longhouse where they were born. When a woman married, her husband came to live with her family.

The Haudenosaunee want to leave the world a good place for future children of the confederacy. They still care about that today.

CHAPTER 4

AFTER THE EUROPEANS

The Haudenosaunee met French explorers in 1609. At first, the French attacked the Haudenosaunee people. But eventually, there was peace and they began to trade with one another. The French traded tools, clothes, and

COMPLETE AN ACTIVITY HERE!

Beaver fur was a popular item to trade.

other goods for furs. Unfortunately, the Haudenosaunee also got European diseases from the French, and many American Indians died.

The Haudenosaunee make beautiful beaded art, such as bags, necklaces, and headpieces.

Long before the Europeans arrived, the Haudenosaunee recorded their history, laws, and traditions with wampum beaded belts. The beads were made from shells through a delicate and complicated process. The belts are still used in **ceremonies** today.

An agreement is spoken while a wampum belt is put together.

Many people believe that the Haudenosaunee's Great League of Peace inspired parts of the US Constitution. Each set of Haudenosaunee laws celebrates the importance of unity and personal success. The US government also organizes leadership in similar ways to the Haudenosaunee.

An agreement between the Iroquois and the US is displayed at the National Museum of the American Indian.

The Smoke Dance is a popular dance performed by Haudenosaunee.

Today there are about 125,000 Haudenosaunee people living in Ontario, Quebec, New York, Wisconsin, and Oklahoma. Few live in longhouses, but they still keep their traditional ways. They are led by Clan Mothers and Chiefs who focus on preserving the confederacy and caring for the **environment**.

MAKING CONNECTIONS

TEXT-TO-SELF

The Haudenosaunee lived in longhouses with many family members. Would you like to share a home with as many people as the Haudenosaunee do? Please explain your answer.

TEXT-TO-TEXT

Have you read another book about an American Indian nation? If so, how is their culture similar to or different from the Iroquois people?

TEXT-TO-WORLD

The Iroquois recorded some of their history in wampum belts. What are other ways history can be recorded without writing?

GLOSSARY

breechcloth — a cloth worn over the groin.

ceremony — a formal event held on a special occasion.

elder — a person having authority because of age or experience.

environment — the natural world, including air, water, land, and animals.

generation — all the people born and living at the same time.

harvest — to gather a crop.

principle — a basic law or truth on which action or behavior is based.

prophet — someone who speaks a message given to them from a higher power.

settler — a person who moves with a group of others to live in a new country or area. A place where settlers live is called a settlement.

INDEX

DiscoverRoo!
ONLINE RESOURCES

This book is filled with videos, puzzles, games, and more! Scan the QR codes* while you read, or visit the website below to make this book pop.

popbooksonline.com/Iroquois

*Scanning QR codes requires a web-enabled smart device with a QR code reader app and a camera.